No One Cares

Writing anything these days to which no would say is rather difficult and would require a really vivid imagination, lucky I came along then.

I like to think outside the box of normality, between two worlds due to my mental illness I live with, both worlds are very different and very real and this is why I believe this will set a kind of precedence within the world of books because it will be one of pure honesty that we only really see these days from the minds an uncorrupted child's mind.

Children are mostly protected from a lot of the worlds dark side that humanity has to offer, so I can hold my head up and tell you everything I've put in this book will be the truth and factually researched because I want to give people an open window into the dark world that I have for years had to live within just to survive long enough to tell this story, I hope it offers people some insight and gives them the strength to stand up and be heard, or stand up for others and make a difference in the world.

What is normal? I consider myself to be normal but from a different perspective perhaps from what other people perceive to be normal,

No One Cares

Normies I consider to be sheeple living in herds like cattle and copying each other bowing to the elected few that lead, born to be controlled by the system doing as their told without questioning those that are telling them how too, people live, breath and are that system without a second thought for fear of being cast out of the great machine, singled out as mad or insane.

Humans existence as part of the third circle theory is to breed, work, pay taxes till they die, that's life and anyone who is seen to fight this system of conformity too human existence is cast out as a madman, medicated and locked away from normie society.

The world I see is a greedy, corrupted, dishonest and untrustworthy society, social media since its birth has escalated this because it gives people a window into our minds, we post all our thoughts when we shouldn't and that leads to arguments between peers and then social issues for the wider communities, constant updates of personal information and then people wonder why trolls and scammers exist in the online world.

No One Cares

There is also a world hidden behind a secret veil of lies, confidentiality especially to do with mental health & children's care systems,

This is how ive somehow managed to turn my negative life around into something more positive as even my psychiatrist seemed quite surprised by, If I am able to do what I've managed then hopefully reading through this will give anyone else going through similar issues will have some hope given to them to do the same, in turn we can make the world a little better and brighter for those in dark places right now.

For me family is more than just a word, it's about sharing with people we live with & sometimes work with or are friends with, spending time together as a family unit and knowing you can rely on each other to be around when we need them, thats what family os for and shouldn't need no rewards for being just that.

I've always felt that I am an enigma, an anomaly, a creation by the system, raised by the system, designed to now help people lost within that same system, but I am not the system and I can live in

No One Cares

accordance to our laws and rules set by society because I choose too.

Ref : Matrix Revolution 2003

"Why do you persist Mr Anderson"

Because I choose to.

A film directed by Andy Wachoski, Lana Wachoski and cast Keanu Reeves, Laurence Fishburne, Carrie-Anne Moss & Hugo Weaving.

The Matrix film I personally believe is a near perfect example of a man having a complete mental breakdown which i can relate too that makes complete sense to me because of his work & other life commitments which I've seen many times causing people to become ill, mentally, the stresses of life can break a mind in which our minds work against us to protect us from ourselves, I believe once a mind breaks it opens a door to the real world we have been conditioned not to see, we collectively choose to ignore it because it would break the system (Matrix) if we did, we become institutionalized by the protection around us, seen often in care,

No One Cares

prison services as people become reliant on those services we forget our independence.

I've met a lot of people in my time and the most honest of those are people who have broken mentally and it's through these people I've learned how to survive and in turn use everything what i've learned to then support others, the student becomes the master, we are all teachers.

Becoming a parent is supposed to be a shared commitment and should be one of the most wonderful and happiest feelings humanity has learned as I have along the way to becoming a father myself, too cherish life, it's about the love of two people, in some cases it's more and they decide to create another life and sharing the nurturing of the child.

With laws dictating that we raise children with a good sense of morals and teaching them right from wrong until they become old enough & experienced enough to look after themselves into adulthood.

No One Cares

Having the power to create does not give people god like powers nor the right to mis-use or abuse those they create, So what on earth went completely wrong in my case?
I've searched everywhere for answers all my life feeling lost and cut off from the world as if I was behind an unbreakable glass wall, People could see me but not hear me nor could I talk to them,
I wanted too for years but I didn't know how for fear of being beaten, which was very often.

I started writing this in my late thirties after getting proper psychiatric help and having good, honest decent support with my mental health issues, which I unknowingly covered over through drug abuse and alcohol, it was only when I stopped these was my mental illness seen for what it is, people began to see i wasn't a monster or a bad apple out to cause trouble, I just needed help because I wasn't raised properly but in fact I was a nice person who had learned a good sense of morals and so my recovery process started and led me to where I am writing this.

My aim is to help others within childrens care services who have had similar experiences to find the power and speak up and for

No One Cares

children who feel they have no voice and for those who feel they are alone in the system that doesn't actually care by the way of warmth of love, being fostered, adopted or cared for by other people than your own parents is more clinical love from a certain point of view, it's to protect first which is much colder and in my case destroyed my childhood.

Care proceedings have an estimated timeframe of forty weeks and concurrent planning is required, and a final care plan is put forward by local authorities is required to provide a plan for permanence whether with parents, family members, long term foster parents or adopters.

I want to focus on what I believe back then was a failed system that was supposed to help a child in need but instead failed on an immense level and in doing so nearly created a monster given the choices presented to a young child I had laid in front of me at those times, which would have lost a citizen whom would add input into society and claim its stake in the human world for all the wrong reasons, because I still believe this system is still broken due to the failings in the deaths of young children in the UK with references to

No One Cares

Baby P, Victoria Climbie and more recently at the time of writing Mikaeel Kular and others
May they all rest in peace.

Before anyone starts to criticize this and tries slating this I have researched about NHS studies of mental health, social services, child protection and from my own experience of my life and also people ive met along the way and also what life was like for me growing up in care due to these mental health conditions affecting not just me but my family and my life.

Schizophrenia is a long-term mental health condition that causes a range of different psychological symptoms including things like :
Hallucinations - Hearing or seeing things that do not exist.
Delusions - Unusual beliefs not based on reality which often contradict the evidence.
Muddled thoughts based on the hallucinations or delusions.
Changes in behaviour.
Doctors often describe schizophrenia as a psychotic illness. This means that sometimes a person may not be able to distinguish their own thoughts and ideas from reality. Schizophrenia is one of the

No One Cares

most common serious mental health conditions. About 1 in 100 people will experience schizophrenia in their lifetime, with many continuing to lead somewhat normal lives.

Schizophrenia is most often diagnosed between the ages of 15 and 35. Men & Women are equally affected, there is no single test for schizophrenia, it is most often diagnosed after an assessment by a mental health care professional, such as a psychiatrist.

It is important that schizophrenia is diagnosed as early as possible, as the chances of recovery improve the earlier it is treated. If schizophrenia is well managed, it is possible to reduce the chances of relapses.
This can include recognizing signs of acute episode, taking medication as prescribed, talking to others about the condition.

There are many charities and support groups offering help and advice on living with schizophrenia, most people find it comforting to talk to others with a similar condition, I found a thing like that called Peer Support, it's a way of supporting other people by using my own lived experiences of what it's like living with a mental health

No One Cares

condition, I've found that by far the best kind of support, because they totally understand, by all means work alongside the professionals but then to all the professionals & local authorities please take note, work with the peer support groups because they really do help, most are non-profit organisations so tend to fund raise and are run by volunteers, using them and supporting & promoting these groups could help reduce our ever growing healthcare / social care budgets.

Personality Disorder is what my diagnosis is, this comes from childhood trauma and is a way for a child to protect themselves, in essence it splits their personality in order to adapt to their ever changing environment, the earlier this is detected and helped with is best in childhood, because by adulthood there is no known cure, there are ways to help, to cope, anti-psych medications which help my thought process slow down but come with a range of side-effects,

I use therapy groups for support, others use things like C.B.T (Cognitive Behavioural Therapy)

Because when you're taught the wrong way of doing things and that way becomes normal for you it's very difficult to unlearn what you've

No One Cares

been taught, if you argue or fight or hit a child they record everything in their heads, it desensitizes them and it can lead to them thinking such behaviours and actions are ok, we imprint ourselves onto our children, so it's our duty, responsibility to ensure we do our job of raising our children the right way.

That's why a parents role as well as the whole community's role is vital in helping to teach the next generation the correct ways of being decent, as well as protecting them, it's not grassing if you suspect a minor is being abused, I say bloody report it!! Let the social services or other authorities do the job they're tasked to do, if they then have no case to answer then that's ok too, but if they intervene based on your reporting and it leads to a child being placed into protective custody then I would applaud anyone who takes that first step to protecting the child.

No one cared enough to do that for me, until it was too late and by then the damage to me & my family was already done, it's completely destroyed everything and left me a mental wreck, but somehow I've survived.

No One Cares

I think back through the support ive had in my later years of life I have got through it all and I am still alive and have even been able to make a life for myself & have a family of my own, so NEVER! GIVE UP! EVER!

There are lots of good people out in the world of social workers, support workers so i'm not blaming an individual in particular, I've been at the point many times of giving up and even attempted to end my life but i don't want to focus on that as this is supposed to be giving people hope and give them the will to go on.

Social workers are a valuable asset to the children that need their help and id offer my support in a heartbeat to these people who do a very hard job at times and im forever grateful to those who tried their best with me, I know i was hard work, constantly running away from different homes and even schools and to all those police officers who do a fantastic job trying to keep me safe even though back then I couldn't see it and fought against them, the people in these roles do them because they care about others, in a sense, isn't that what superheroes are about?

No One Cares

Using their powers for the greater good of the human race giving us hope that one day we can also do these roles and become like them.

I had quite a few social workers in my time and my blame lies with the system itself at the time, I felt it was flawed and vulnerable children like myself slipped through its safety net and this is my stake to the world in an effort to put right what once went wrong and undo what was done.

Real names have been changed in order to protect people's identities other than my own.

A lot of the rules and good practices of any child care system are designed to protect children from physical and sexual abuse, mental torture from all walks of life, in England, Wales, Scotland & Ireland, there never has been a statutory obligation to report alledged child abuse to the police, however both the children act 1989 and 2004 makes clear statutory obligation on all professionals to report suspected child abuse.

No One Cares

Some can be unknown to victims, some are even family members that have been known to do these horrible acts against a defenceless and vulnerable children in their care of guardianship, I understand this could upset a few people but I at the point in life that's not my problem to deal with, people need to learn what happened and what ive witnessed, lived through and survived through, these things unfortunately do still happen even today, I've wittness'ed an ever increasing amount of known pedophiles being caught out by hunting groups and i see on social media that another child was failed by the system supposed to be protecting them when they needed help and support.

Some of these cases I refer too ended in deaths because the physical abuse was so severe, and we as a supposedly civilised society and community need to do more to protect all children from these animals, Yes i am somewhat bitter towards these people because what they do destroys the child both physically and mentally and we have a very weak justice system, I think we need a tougher system of punishment for people who hurt children, none of this ten year offenders register, make it life.

No One Cares

My father from what i've learned suffered from his mental disorder for many years, some with success and others without, on medication throughout his life and also in and out of hospital, I found him working on hospital grounds selling candles when I first met him after many years trying to find him, thinking back I guess social services were trying to protect me as i asked them many times to help me locate his whereabouts.

Everytime i asked they always seemed to fob me off or tried to delay me searching for him by giving me false hopes that they were doing their best to find him.

In some parts I don't regret finding him because his actions when I did made me realise i didn't need him, but sometimes these things need doing just so we know and can learn from it, it's called lived experience and is by far the best teaching method ever known to mankind.

No One Cares

Studies show that children who have an involved father are more likely to be emotionally secure, be confident to explore their surroundings as they grow older, have better social connections with peers, their children are also less likely to get into trouble at home, school, or in the neighbourhood.

Infants who receive high levels of affection from their fathers (e.g babies whose fathers respond quickly to their cries and who play together) are more securely attached, that is they can explore their environment comfortably when a parent is nearby and can readily accept comfort from their parent after a brief separation. A number of studies suggest they are also more sociable and popular with other children throughout early childhood.

The way fathers play with their children also has an important impact on a child's emotional and social development, Fathers spend a much higher percentage of their one-on -one interaction with infants and preschoolers in stimulating playful activities than mothers do, from these interactions, children learn how to regulate their feelings and behaviours, roughhousing with dad for example

No One Cares

can teach a child how to deal with aggressive impulses and physical contact without losing control of their emotions, Generally speaking.

Fathers also tend to promote independence and an orientation to the outside world, fathers often push achievement while mothers stress nurturing, both of which are important to a healthy development for the child, as a result children who grow up with involved fathers are more comfortable exploring the world around them and are more likely to exhibit self control and pro social behaviour.

In short, fathers can have a powerful and positive impact upon the development and health of children.

My father from what I know suffered with schizophrenia all my life, his life was in & out of hospital, I know the BBC did a documentary on mental illness some years ago and my dad was one of those on the program, he lived alone most of his life with little or no friends that I'm aware of, He died in the company of just my brother whom I don't speak to, I've always been worried if I would end up like him so did some research into mental health, I recently learned he had

No One Cares

passed away but as mixed up as my family is no one saw fit to even inform me, so I have no way of knowing or finding out where he was buried without any information to go on the agencies I asked around couldn't release any information.

My own biological brother saw fit to threaten me for even asking about it.

To anyone who has parents I can honestly say respect them for all they do for you, they may be tough on you, tell you no from time to time, but they do it because they love you, care for you, they have a moral & legal obligation as your parent to raise you with good morals and a sense of identity, the rest you make up together, because not having that is like watching from across a vast, empty canyon and not being able to be a part of it, seeing your fathers being a dad to you, it kills me inside but I am happy for you, On a positive note it does drive me to be as best a dad can be towards my own children, to be there when they need me.

My brother has spent a large number of years in prison for armed robbery, kidnapping and I also heard an allegation of rape, as well as having a number of firearms and the company of associates he

No One Cares

keeps are of the gangster culture, so I consider my brother a risk to be around, We fell out because I asked him to remove the guns when I invited him to stay, he instead acted as if in prison and threatened me, I involved the police and they let me know there was a warrant out to arrest him, so they picked him up from the nightclub he was working at and ended up back in prison for around two years, we've never spoken since.

I was in the care system twice in my entire lifetime before eighteen, The first time I was around six months old, according to my mother in conversations we've had, my father's illness caused him to physically abuse me, a number of attempts to end my life, putting glass in my cot, and even broke my nose for being a noisy baby as I lay in a pram, Who on earth does that to a baby?

As well as mistreating my mother who I wish to protect so I won't be disclosing who she is.

My mother was just trying to protect her children from a misunderstood illness in a person while she was being beaten and abused by this man placed upon my birth certificate.

I know he lived on medications and spent most of his time around hospital, even sectioned a few times and lived in a pokey little flat

No One Cares

alone, old age creeping in, no real friends or family around at the time of writing this, I have spoken to him twice in my entire lifetime but never got any answers from him, I found out where he was living when I was seventeen.

I spent a few years in care with foster parents from six months old, I remember things from when I was four years old, sitting on the stairs of the three bedroom house waiting for the postman to deliver the mail, I was waiting for my birthday card to arrive, it was August nineteen seventy nine, as far as this child knew these people were my parents, my mum & dad, I remember going to school, I'm presuming nursery, infants and on sundays me & my "dad" would go to the airport to watch planes land and take off whilst "mum" cooked a roast dinner, then as a family we would go visit granny who lived a short walk away, she always let us pick apples from her tree, as far as I remember life was good as long as I behaved.

As a child watching these great machines do what they do was an awesome sight to behold and this was the first time I'd ever seen a plane as well as spending time with what I thought was my father, it was the best feeling in the whole world and if I think back on my life

No One Cares

I can honestly say that was the only point of my life I've ever felt "normal" . Life was great or so I thought.

My biological brother lived with us, so again I can only presume behind the scenes social services had placed my brother in care with us when he was born.
I'm one & half years older then my brother so I wouldn't have been aware of what's going on, I just know I had a brother younger than me, we were taught discipline in a hard style but I came to respect it of sorts.

After an hour of holding out your arms with the old style yellow pages book placed upon them and you wasn't allowed to drop your arms for fear of getting a beating with the belt was pure torture for a minor, but he was my "dad" ,

Another time my "dad" left me outside a prison at the bus stop after saying if I ever get into trouble with the police this is where I would end up, he then walked off and ordered me to stay there, I kept staring at the prison walls which to a child were massive, thankfully I've never been to prison, Ever!

No One Cares

I looked around for my "dad" and couldn't see him anywhere, I got scared, I cried, you can't imagine what that does to a child's mind but my "dad" used a lot of ways to scare us into behaving, and even resorted to using a belt when we was naughty, I remind you this I now know years later was my foster parents.

I must have been around five years old I was at school and my dad always picked us up and we walked home, me and my brother shared a bedroom, we had posters of planes the "Red Baron" a famous bi-plane was my favourite, as a child I had dreams of owning one so I could fly away to a better place, from these horrible people, yes we had good days.
Things were very strict and children were never to question an adult or their behaviour, at least that's what i learned so i didn't even attempt to do anything that would warrant a reprisal.

I remember enjoying school, doing normal things like children do, playing, painting, having fun and learning, since all this has happened i'm now in favour of home schooling children because i

No One Cares

believe our education system is flawed by its own arrogance towards change, its so stuck in its agendas to tick boxes that its forgetting its purpose, children need to be learning how to balance a bank account, how to pay taxes, VAT and invoices, how to hold and maintain relationships and respect within the communities they all live in, we just fire fight after the fact every sibgle time, children misbehave so they bring in anti-social asbos but all its done is lose respect for our laws, the amout of drugs i see nowadays being peddled by the youth is far worse than what i grew up around and i took a lot of drugs, even the new drugs like spice are bloody scary ive seen what that does to people and think are they stupid, but i also see a lot of people forcing it upon them, sometime just for a laugh as they watch the already vulnerable person fall into a monged state of nothing more than a dribbling, tripped out mess, ive seen a lot of clips from prisoners who seem to have access to phones who record such incidents, theres no consistancy in this country anymore, you all say we want to do this but no one ever follows through, its all vote winning policies and back patting from do-gooders who want to nothing but look good for their peers.

No One Cares

One day however my dad seemed really angry towards me as he picked me up from school, this went on into the evening, we were about the dinner I remember it was cold & dark outside and noticed my dad had run a bath with what I now know was freezing cold water.

My dad grabbed my arm as I sat at the table hurting me in the process and placed me into the bath fully clothed, what he did next still haunts me to this day, he turned the light off so it was very dark, my dad tried to drown me, I struggled and feared for my life, what did I do as a five year old to make my "dad" want to try and kill me? I screamed, I choked and gasped for air when he allowed me to surface.

He pushed on me again and pushed my head back under the water a few times, then my "mum" came in and said enough! I was allowed to get dry and that was that, I never dared ask nor was told why he did this even to this day, I hope this offers an understanding as to why I distrust people because I still feel the real me died that night & something else now lives within me, how can I trust anyone or love anyone who wants to hurt me, I lived with them in pure fear of it happening again, my trust in these two was completely gone,

No One Cares

my foster mother knew what was happening and did absolutely nothing to stop it, I could have been dead for all she knew, I've grown up with that view if you stand by and do nothing to help then you should be held accountable too, people like that make me physically sick, those who hurt or abused children.

A regular visitor I only knew him as Mr Penny but after some extensive research I later found out he was a family solicitor, I presume he looked in on me & my brother from time to time too see how we were doing, He was great! A very happy & jolly character with their own office not too far away, which happened to be near where we went food shopping at the civic centre, when I think back now it was to see my mother who kept trying to get her sons back out of care.

By then my real mother had escaped from my real father and had met someone else whom I now know was our step-father, she was now fighting the care system to regain her boys.
We used to always go in my foster dads car to these meetings, as a child I was completely oblivious to what was really going on, children are innocent and it's us adults who impact onto them, we all

No One Cares

have a duty to ensure the safeguarding and moral standing of raising a child is upheld.

I'm unsure what went on behind the scenes because as a small child no one ever told you anything grownup or updated you with how social workers and things happen, this has happened many times in my life, I'm told my mother fought tooth & nail against the court's ruling of placing me in care to get me back, but the next thing I knew was that we were moving to a new house, far away from our old one.

We moved to Warrington, A big lorry turned up one morning, the house filled with packed boxes with all our belongings, I don't remember the cats name but I was worried about our cat missing at the time, we had to return a few days later to pick it up, the neighbours had taken it in and got in contact, so with cat in box we left and headed along the motorway to our new house.

We each had our own rooms, filled with toys and that was the last I saw of my mother, the unusual meetings were completely stopped, being a young child I never questioned any of it.

No One Cares

I started a new school, made new friends and even learned to walk to school with my younger brother without our foster mum, I got into trouble because I kept eating my packed lunch on the way to school, as well as being a normal child.

We had a neighbour who worked for Wimpy, a fast food chain and made friends with the family, he always brought us little gifts, I made friends at school and I'll always remember being in the school play, they made a big stage and I had to rehearse a lot as I was a windup toy soldier.

My foster parents & even my brother as well as the whole school came to watch and life seemed to start feeling good once more, every friday our foster dad took us to the shop to buy sweets and a comic for being good, when we weren't good out came the leather belt but I became a very fast learner to the tough discipline, I went out with my foster dad & my brother went out mainly with my foster mother unless it was for food shopping then we all went together.

No One Cares

Where we lived, we had a small wooded area that we had to walk through to get to the main shops, the shopping centre was massive, filled with multiple shops, one winter whilst walking to these shops my brother wore an old duffle coat with his hands in his pockets to keep warm, where it had been snowing it was slippery, my brother fell flat on his face, I laughed my head off as he his face and a tooth had burst through his lip for which he needed stitches to fix.

I still cringe even years later when people hurt themselves, I can't handle blood or broken bones or bits missing from a person.

My foster mother was walking back from shopping (we did a lot of shopping) I helped carry the bags and remember we had to cross a great big arched bridge and it was still snowing, we used to have a lot of decent snow in my youth, so again it was slippery and my foster mother fell over, I couldn't contain my laughter as im sure no one would be able to as a young child.

A child's laughter should never be contained as it possesses such immense power.

No One Cares

I got into trouble for laughing and got a slap for my efforts, when i got home out came the belt again for what I thought at the time I was just being myself, so that beating taught me to hide my true self to protect myself from further beatings, even today in two thousand & nineteen I still subconsciously do that, I began to build a mental brick wall around me, a mental prison in my head shutting off the outside world, they may break my bones & hurt me but they won't ever get into my head, what child on earth has to do this in order to survive? It's a disgrace that any child should even have to think about this let alone do this.

A couple more years of living with these horrible people, I was so broken inside, withdrawn, I mistrusted every adult, I became ill but I don't know what, but I know I was very sick with a fever & a doctor had to come out and visit, I had to stay in bed for many days, I asked my foster mother if I was dying because no one told me what was wrong with me.

I got better and life went back to normality with me playing the game of not getting caught being a pain, or being a normal child scared of what could happen if I cause trouble, I didn't understand time so a

No One Cares

week felt like a lifetime, if you're unhappy that week can seem like an eternity & no one to talk to about my problems, none that I felt I could talk too, not even a teacher.

I was in junior school then suddenly life changed, out of the blue both my foster mum and dad sat me & my brother down and said me & him were going away, but they didn't say where.

As a child who's gone through this I can honestly say I thought id had upset my parents and they were sending me away for being bad or because they didn't love us anymore, I was distraught to say the least, too where I wondered, then cried the whole time, Mr Penny the solicitor came and picked us up, he told us that our foster parents wasn't our real parents, I was so confused, my whole world had exploded into tiny pieces, I continued crying & hugged my foster mum asking what did we do wrong that's led us to being taken away, my foster mother didn't say anything she just hugged me.

Now i'm sorry but what on earth do you think that does to a child & his mind, my whole world had been destroyed in one sentence, in the back of the car I looked back to wave goodbye to my parents

No One Cares

and suddenly they were gone as we turned the corner, gone out of sight and me off to a life of yet even more misery, pain & abuse.

My head was all over the place, I was around seven by now, my mind & thoughts racing, Mr Penny told us "You're going home to your real mum" my reply was that I thought my foster parents were our mum & dad, the conversation ended there.

We ended up on an estate with very big highrise flats, a lady was stood on the path and Mr Penny said, "This is your mum" , as we got out of the car my mother gave me the biggest hug id ever had in my life and we went into the flat to meet my other family.

Mam had a new fella by now after escaping from my dad and they had children who are technically my half-siblings, we had a small garden fenced in being a bottom floor flat.
Summers were baking hot & long, the first night with this new family I was given alcohol to drink (I was seven) I drank it but later it made me sick.

No One Cares

I was not prepared for this new life at all as a young child, being beaten and abused by those that are supposed to love you and care for you leaves a mark upon you, they are not visible scars, they are mental & as far as I know people can't see into your head, I was so messed up by now id learned to cut off from my emotions completely & became afraid to talk to these new people who were said to be my real parent/s, I couldn't trust what anyone said to me anymore, that damage was already done, this wasn't my mum I thought and my step-dad wasn't my dad, I've been placed with strangers with no way out by a social worker who was supposed to be looking out for me.

My mother did teach me to write using dotted lines, I learned in just a single night, fast learner skills through fear is not how to teach children, and I went to school not too far away, over time things became more settled however my stepdad was drinking very heavily and daily now and took it upon himself to start hitting & fighting with my mother almost every day that I can remember, I was constantly woken many nights having to listen as a child too my mother crying or screaming and the sounds of thuds of her being hit, I lay under my covers fearing the monster would come in and attack me fearing

No One Cares

for my life crying myself to sleep, after what my foster dad had done over my early years I had become so afraid of all adults and started to wet the bed, this unfortunately led to more beatings.

It soon became clear me & my brother didn't fit in with this family and we were treated as outsiders, animals were treated better than us.

I even had to steal food from the fridge just to eat when everyone else was asleep, I used to eat a lot of bread because they didn't seem to notice that missing out of fear of being beaten again and steal tins of food, I still eat some foods straight out of a tin even today, it's ingrained into my head as normal,

We were regularly stripped naked and ridiculed and forced to do stupid shit in front of other family members, they even dressed me up as a girl , forced makeup on me and told me to go to the pub across the road, if we didn't do as told they got really angry at us and that resulted in more beatings, we were forced to go and play in a field across the road, we had no toys so had to use our imagination, we spent many days living in a fantasy world to escape our reality of pain, abuse & hatred, I still play a lot of online games

No One Cares

to escape reality because I still struggle with it, I see patterns in systems and people, I play in the background and learn tactics very fast, I once reached the top 25K in the whole global market considering around 70 million or so bought a certain online game, i'm a perfectionist now, i get angry with myself if i get things wrong, its all or nothing with me, theres no middle ground, I speak truths that some may not like but you can't really argue with the truth.

No parent or guardian has a right to beat a child for fun or their entertainment, anyone who does is sick in the head and isn't worthy of the title "Parent" and we as a collective must do all we can to combat any suspected forms of abuse, if we do nothing then you leave that child with the prospect of being someone like I am, broken, wild, living in an isolated existence.

My three older step-sisters lived with us, the eldest was the boss in the absence of my parents out drinking but she was always busy with her boyfriend at the time, I don't remember the middle sister being around much so it fell to the last of the three to look after us, she used to feed us and made sure we got to school, times were

No One Cares

tough with nine of us living in the three bed flat but it was a big old place not like these modern pokey flats in today's markets.

I spent many days locked in my bedroom, there was a lock attached outside so bedwetting became normal for me with no access to a toilet, a child who is scared to talk will not ask for even simple things out of fear but this seemed to push my step-dad to the limit and he began to beat me, as I lay on the bed crying he picked me up by the ankles and he held me out of the second floor window, upside down. He told me if I pissed the bed again he will drop me, so I continued to live in absolute fear of these people that were supposed to care for me & constantly beaten, daily and abused for their entertainment when angry or bored, I felt empty like a shell, nothing more than a punchbag.

I began stealing from school, biscuits and other items, a form of kleptomania because I had nothing, I still collect comics and other stuff, so I was fast becoming a rebel getting into trouble and made regular trips to see the headmaster, I may as well have had my desk in their, I was made to sit in a classroom on my own because I

No One Cares

wouldn't behave at the dinner table, I plastered my school pudding all over everyone else's work books and sat at my table again.

I just sat there staring into nothing, filled with rage, after everything that had gone on and no one to turn too, I was starting to lose control of myself & my anger, I had a hatred for people, no one was giving me any sense of doing what's right & at the same time telling me to always be good. By way of being scared into doing as im told, I was so mixed up & confused I needed help but no one ever came and I was too afraid to ask anyone and suffered in silence crying myself to sleep wishing I could die, so alone in the darkness of my own mind.

Somehow I had formed some kind of attachment to my mother even with all this hatred I felt pity for her being beaten by my dad, then my step-dad, although i don't know how, she was my mum and im supposed to lover her & she love me, I was in school and one of the class children's mother had passed away, our class was told that this child would be off for some time yet all I could think about was wishing it was me, wishing I could swap places with her so I could be free of this evil person who kept hurting me.

No One Cares

It left me wondering what is the meaning to die, what is this thing i've heard of but I had no previous knowledge of death left unanswered questions and later in life I guess gave me in some weird sense a fascination with death and demons & devils.

A lad in my class I wont say who belittled a picture I made for my mother during lessons, I am filled with rage suddenly filled my head as I stood at the table I picked up a pair of scissors and held them tightly but all I heard in my head was another adult about to beat me and shouting abuse at me in visions my mind was making up, some of the other children came over to see what was going on and asked if i was ok so i told them all to go away and leave me alone looking them directly in their eyes like some kind of psychotic killer, my eyes burned into their skin as my rage inside grew and in my head they were all laughing at me.

The lad who belittled my picture stood a little away from me so I turned towards him and threw the scissors towards him in a fit of rage and screamed "Dont you slag my mother off" .

I know it's a hard thing to understand because I wouldn't wish it on any child to get hurt but the scissors hit him right on the bridge of his

No One Cares

nose, it was a perfect shot and blood spilled out across the classroom. The class erupted into chaos "SIR" the children all shouted as the blood streamed down the child's face, the teacher looked up then seemed to panic as the chaos continued.

I stood like a person possessed over the bleeding child who was sat on the floor by now I said "Slag my mother off again and I'll kill you", I honestly look back and think I had totally lost the plot, almost psychotic, i was only around seven or eight years old, I felt like a monster, exactly like the ones I feared, people would fear me instead, it gave me power, that's what it felt like.

What had I become, perhaps just like my father like I feared I would, but for the first time in my life I felt like I had power over people instead of them having power over me, a very dangerous situation for any child to contemplate, it stopped me feeling like a victim but in gaining this power i had hurt another child, not something to be proud of I know that now, the teacher told me i was suspended immediately and he marched me home straight away, the teacher banged on the door and explained what happened in school, my mother wears a lot of rings then punched me full force in the face

No One Cares

with her fist in front of the teacher, it left me with the biggest black eye ive ever had, I couldn't see out of my eye for weeks, no one ever checked it to see if it was ok.

I had bruises all over my body, burns from her fags that she did on purpose and locked in my bedroom for days on end and starved, I dont know if i deserved it for what i did but its completely crippled my way of thinking about this world.

I started to run away, I learn things fast, I learned how to open my locked door and sneaked out, I just wanted to get away from these people and when i did i felt freedom for the first time, it was like euphoria washing over you, it was amazing and in the middle of the night, no one else was out, I wasn't scared at all.

I didn't care about anyone anymore I followed some train tracks for a few hours dodging the oncoming trains and waited till they passed by before continuing until I reached a tunnel, I waited for the next train to pass then I ran as fast as I could through the tunnel, I managed to get to the other side but there was a very steep

No One Cares

embankment on the left side, so I tried to climb it and thankfully got off the tracks.

I must have missed the next train by around ten seconds or so, I just sat there on the bank watching the train whizz past, I was beginning to get a sense of euphoria again, the adrenaline pumping through my body, I almost felt like superman, invincible, I had no fear of some situations that could have resulted in my own death.

For two days I walked and walked aimlessly to nowhere and what must have been miles by now i thought id left the big city I was in yet somehow i still remained within its limits not a great distance from where I lived, but to a child with no knowledge of surroundings I could have been the other side of the world, I hid in the city centre sleeping behind some bins that a business used, cold and lonely but free from the monsters who abused me.

I sat there thinking to myself what would people say should anyone find me or if I would ever in fact be found, was anyone even looking for me or had not bothered at all, I know now the police force was out in force looking for me, I even made the papers and the news at 10 on TV.

No One Cares

However if i saw a police car or van i walked the other way scared they would return me to the monsters called parents, starving, dehydrated I was alive somehow on my last bit of energy I found what I remember was a football pitch on an estate, I hadn't a clue where I was, I was completely lost and lost all sense of direction, I was vulnerable and i think the lads playing football at the time saw the state I was in and came over to speak to me.

I don't remember much of the conversation with them but i do know they took me to the youth club and because I told them I had ran away the adults informed the police straight away, whilst we waited i was given food and water, the food was tough to eat after not eating for days, my throat began to burn so I drank the water to help, within about ten minutes or so the police arrived and i saw them speaking to the adults I was totally oblivious to anything going on or the commotion I had caused by running away.

The police officer walked up to me and asked me to confirm what he had been told, afraid i was in trouble i told him i ran away, he asked if I was Pete i nodded and replied "Yes" looking confused as to how he knew my name, then the officer escorted me to his police car as

No One Cares

he radioed in, he asked if everything was ok and that if I said anything it would still be ok, But i couldn't trust any adults, i live with regret now in later years I so wish id had the courage to have spoken up to the officer and told him everything that had happened, my life would have been so different, but i didn't i was afraid of all adults and the fear began creeping back in as i knew he was taking me home to the place I dreaded, I lied and said I was fine……..Arrrrgh!!!

It was getting dark by the time the officer and I returned to my home and as we pulled up in his patrol car the fear had once again consumed me, the first person I saw was my mother.
She cried and hugged me then shouted at me saying to never do that again, I watched the news and saw there was around seventy-five officers out looking for me over the last couple of days, i was made some food as a reporter from the local paper came round taking photos as I sat and ate a plate of sausage, mash and beans, I was starving.

I always remember that day they asked me where I was, I replied I was walking around and got lost and forgot the way home, I couldn't

No One Cares

dare say i had ran away, for a few days after returning home everything seemed normal and i felt like the local celebrity as everyone had heard of my events via the papers or news, my mum actually spent time with me and spoke to me like I was her son giving me cuddles and kisses, it didn't last longer than a week, it was soon back to the slipper on the hands or slapped in the face and beaten with her fist and treated like an animal or a slave, sent on errands to the shop, cleaning the house from top to toe, I felt like an animal and not someone's son.

I went back into my shell, scared to ask for food so I stole it again all because I feared upsetting the people who were supposed to be caring for me, people who I thought was treating me how kids were supposed to be treated, after getting another regular beating i had to rebuild the mental prison in my mind and i lived in my head whilst my body walked around like a soulless dummy lost to the outside world.

I hear voices ask "why didn't you ever say something to someone" and tell them what was happening, all i can say is how can any child think that what a parent is doing is wrong when they're supposed to

No One Cares

be our teachers of life, how can anyone think a child who is beaten daily has the confidence to question this if no one tells them they're allowed too.

We as a civilised society of human beings have a duty of responsibility to safeguard children from all walks of life are kept safe and if we think otherwise, then we have a moral duty to inform either a police officer or social worker, even a teacher who can take the necessary steps to intervene, anyone who doesn't do that and instead looks the other way is as bad as the abuser in my books.

How many peadophiles have been caught then later it comes out that the people around them all looked the other way, you all disgust me who do that, no child should ever have to suffer at the hands of abuse, doesn't matter if it's physical, sexual or any other kinds of abuse, it's wrong!

Knowing all that as yourselves the first question again "why didn't I" I so wish I had, ive had to live with that regret all my life, it's eaten away at me from the inside through my teens into adulthood, and it's possibly why it's led me to doing this , my book i want to help other

No One Cares

people in similar situations to feel they will be listened too, they won't be ignored and someone will protect them if necessary.

The future needs to change for children, every child deserves their basic human rights to be upheld and allows a child to speak up about bad things happening to them even if its because of parents, and anyone who suspects this should report it to be then actioned upon immediately by local authorities, the modern term is safeguarding but there's still a community wide attitude of the term of "grassing" on known mates that needs to change, I personally don't care who gets offended by this but if it's any of my associates they know i would report them as we have on two seperate occasions and i would expect the same approach from the wider community, if I suspected someone was hurting your child i would report it straight away.

A child grows and idolises these people without question and its this part of us that makes us different to some of the worlds animals, it's an emotion we learn yet some people forget what it means, the word "Love" it is the parents responsibility to nurture these children and teach them to love and respect each other, mine however had failed me and only taught me to fear and hate people and even

No One Cares

today i struggle to show any emotions or affection because I don't know how, and even to the point someone once told me i have no personality, I know now what my diagnosis means, i kept it hidden to protect myself and for years it became my normal way of living and coping, it's called survival.

Time went on, so did the daily beatings, they became so normal they didn't hurt any more, I still laugh today if im hurt, I kept running away as that was my way to escape and it became a vicious cycle of being found, return home, beaten for my efforts and life continued till I reached high school, the only thing I learned in high school was how to forge my report card between my parents and teachers, both parties were oblivious until a meeting was called because I had been on report so much, I never finished my second year at high school, I was placed back into care on a care order and would remain in care until I reach eighteen years of age.

Growing up in care is not at all like on TV shows, yes you had staff members and to me it felt like a borstal prison, every part of your life was mapped out, was done for you and you didn't have a say in anything, i wasn't put through school and stayed home all day

No One Cares

playing and dossing about trying to amuse myself, my rage issues rose its head once again and i began to fight the system and the staff members, social workers tried boarding school, I did enjoy that and even joined the football team and made friends but then got into a fight with one lad then i was kicked out, it began by being passed from pillar to post.

Home to home all the time id rage at anyone who tried to break my mental walls I had built to protect myself, no one could handle my outbursts, i was a danger to them as well as myself, i constantly ran away and never settled anywhere too long, until social service i think had enough of me and shipped me off to a home in a rural setting down south, a children's home on farmland with a working farm, the home seemed cut off from the outside world, even housed a football pitch, swimming pool that all the houses used at separate times, the houses were split in accordance to age and had their own staff teams and each child was nominated a key worker from those teams.

I had become so institutionalised, reliant on the services that look after you, people in care or prison can suffer from this, as i had spent three or so years there, most went home for holiday periods

No One Cares

except me and a couple of others, I had a psychologist do studies on me but they couldn't break my mental wall, i did activities , even quite enjoyed some, such as rock climbing, canoeing, even went on an activity holiday, camping, windsurfing, they had educational buildings but never enforced education onto the children, I loved playing with lego, I was possibly much younger mentally then I was but education didn't interest me in the slightest, I was not able to look after myself physically or emotionally, i had to be bathed by force because I hit out at anyone because I hated the world, the staff used restraint methods using force to pin a child to the floor sometimes three or four staff members at a time until the rage episodes had passed.

I bit, I punched, I spat, I swore, i was a wild animal, I fought everyone and everything that didn't go my way, I was the monster what could hurt people if left unchecked, had I been an adult i dare say i could or would have killed someone in that current state, just twelve with a mental age below that.

I felt lost, unloved by the world then everything popped and i cut my wrists and even tried to hang myself a few times but obviously failed in killing myself, i goaded others to run away with me and became

No One Cares

an instigator for troubles at the home, i was no longer the rebel i was the influencer, getting people to join in, i was evicted from the home and moved back to my city of birth, the home had given up on me like everyone else in this forsaken world, i had even given up on myself, but everytime it happened i felt like i had won, they couldn't handle my rage, that unfortunately teaches the child the wrong message, you have to stick it out, when they rage you will find it so much easier to break those mental blocks they have in place, but no one stayed around long enough for that to happen to me.

A child doesn't care for material items, they crave a parents love or affection, I hug my sons and daughters as often as I can just to let them know I love them, they're at an age now for them it's a bit weird for their image for a parent to be hugging their children so they try not too, so I hope they understand I respect that but I still need them all
as much as they need me.

Foster parents for the better part are people who do a fantastic job and service for children needing their care and support within the system, but then every person in this world is different and not

No One Cares

everyone is as nice and not every home is safe, shipped off to an older ladies home I can only describe as the worst kinds of people, improper checks in regards to my safety and the safety of other children in their care.

I felt I had been dumped there, I had an older foster brother and soon got to grips and again I settled in, things were going nicely until I met a local family of lads.

I got into a fight with the youngest, he was around my age this led to them constantly bullying me whenever i went out and i'll be honest they don't realise how close they were to being murdering one of them,

I used to walk around with a big knife hidden under my jacket, I even tried to coerce someone to get them to a certain point in order to do the crime, thankfully I never ran into them when I had it, I could be telling this from a different perspective, people need to understand what bullying, abuse does to the victims, what it does to their thinking, i was already broken from previous life experiences, I wasn't about to let a bunch of children stop me.

No One Cares

I look back on that and I think it's why i'm like I am now, im scared of what i could do to people if I lose control, so I have to keep myself in check but the more I open up to my emotions I feel like I'm losing control of them, it's actually scary sometimes, I get anxious over what you may think are silly things, im security conscious, almost OCD with things like that, I don't let anyone into my little circle, no one knows the real me, so i hope when they all read this they won't think badly of me.

The bullies crowd me, punched me, beat me to the floor, but I never cried, i learned to take my punches till i didn't drop to the floor anymore, i learned to take my punches and then started to give them back, kick a dog every day and one day it bites back, people can be nasty to each other for no other reason than power over another.

Living in care you meet a lot of other children who have come from all kinds of backgrounds and i guess you forge some sort of bond and understanding and empathy towards each other, I feel it was mixing with these people that saved me, i reached thirteen and soon turned to drugs.

No One Cares

I learned how to roll a spliff and regular bought the resin form of weed, we used to get vodka from local store either adults would buy it for us or we stole it, all of it was easy access even to a minor back then, I was fast becoming a complete arse in life, if i wasn't pissed i was stoned, i found a way to escape the mental torture still in my head, i started to get myself arrested, this just gave me a whole new system to fight against and gave me a way to release my anger that had built up inside of me.

Police officers do their job to serve the public and protect all citizens and are a valuable asset, they all do a brilliant job and I have to thank them for keeping me safe during my difficult period in life, although they were keeping me safe, I saw them as the enemy that I could fight back against, I no longer cared what i did, nor who I hurt i turned to crime to pay for my drugs, which was weed, LsD, Speed, i even had gas and other aerosols for a quick buzz all whilst still drinking literally every day.

That's when i met a good friend Leo, that's his real name because he died a long time ago now, we got up to all sorts of trouble, i'm not going to incriminate myself and a few times there was police

No One Cares

involved, one night however i'll never forget, Leo asked me to get into the car he had stolen, i was hungry so I was at the local chippy waiting for food i said no to him, maybe another time I would have, we made arrangements to meet up next day and he drove off, i didn't realise that was the last time i'd ever see my best friend again, he had wrapped the car round a lamp post and killed himself, i didn't find out till the next morning, I couldn't go to his funeral as his mum thought i was a bad influence on her son, i didn't argue with her but it was her son who gave me confidence, i walked to the spot where he died, i felt i had lost a good friend, someone had left a card so i read it in my head and said goodbye to my friend.

I look back on a few times in my life when I could have died, and it makes me believe I am here for something important, what I am here to do comes down to purpose, I believe I am here to help people, teach people and pass on my life experiences so these things can be discussed more openly and I live in hope to change a world that I didn't care about living in, into a world I do care to live in, be the change in the world if you don't see that change.

I have spent many hours under the influence of LsD, Cannabis, Sniffing gas and other aerosols and other drugs, I used them to

No One Cares

escape from reality, I didn't care if I killed myself through this, I struggled to form proper relationships and used people to gain what I could.

I was a monster in a bottle waiting to pop open and burst, I tried my luck at robbing a shop but in making such a racket getting onto the roof, the owners heard and defended their property with force, and beat the crap out of me, I deserved that one, a person should be able to defend their property from anyone attempting to invade their personal space, They broke my arm with a wooden hockey stick as I attempted to defend myself and then they threw me off the roof, I was so thankful when the police arrived to arrest me, but instead they took me to the hospital, I was in hospital for days afterwards, my own fault, my social worker and foster mother helped minimise the trouble I was in with the police.

The police force despite my issues with them throughout my life I respect each and every single officer who does that job to protect all citizens in our country, they're a valuable asset and I have to thank them for keeping me safe from myself over the years, at the time they were the enemies of my own misguided teachings by corrupt

No One Cares

people, and I'm sorry for all the abuse I threw at every officer who dealt with me.

The next part of this story is what still haunts me to this day and is possibly what drives my stance towards a certain kind of people, it may be difficult to read or speak of but I am sorry these things needs to be told because ive had to live with it in my head for years.

There is abuse that goes on within children's services that goes on untold and un-noticed too those in the care system by those very people that are supposed to be caring for that child.
There was an incident mentioned to a foster parent but she completely refused to believe it and dismissed it as utter crap, afterwards I was tormented in ways to keep my mouth shut which resulted in constant beatings setup by these people through their family members, I had no one listening to me, no one I could turn too.

People may ask why didn't you do anything to help or tell someone who would listen, I hope when you read through this you can understand why, ive had to live with this and have questioned it

No One Cares

myself every day, it drove me mad to the point I cut my wrist and ended up in hospital, the cuts weren't deep but I was a novice at that and several more attempts over the years I have tried to leave this planet, I was weak and already broken in my mind but I guess it's part of the reason why i do what i do now by way of support work, helping people with benefits, outing any abuse and have a zero tolerance towards any pedophiles.

I listen to many professionals saying the people who do that have a mental condition,
I totally disagree! because they make a choice to do what they do, they know it's wrong so they try to cover up their antics, that would be like saying people with a mental disorder are dangerous and should be avoided.
I believe in most cases a person with a mental disorder would possibly hurt themselves before others, you're more at risk from people on the street through bullying than a mentally ill person.

To think no one would listen to a child in the care system is a very lonely place to live and it's taken years to overcome that part of my life to where I am today.

No One Cares

After this incident that took place I overheard a conversation between my foster parent and their sister discussing that she would take me on as my foster parent, because it paid well apparently.

My life was worth more than just money thanks, people didn't want me because they cared about me, they just wanted the money that came from having me around, so i'm glad i ran away again, I fully support having checks on anyone in services that provide support in some way but these are still quite new and I still discredit that they only highlight known offences, so if a person hasn't been caught then in the eyes of law they're still deemed safe to be around children, People like Ian Huntley, Jimmy Saville and many others in positions of responsibility around child abuse that trust and power to hurt children in ways I'd care not mention, what angers me even more is the people around them who when it comes out have looked the other way or refused to accept the truths because of who they are or what their status is in life.

What about the children? What about the victims?

No One Cares

A child's life is worth more than money and I became angry with all these people and this led to me robbing my foster parents daughters house with one of my foster sisters on several occasions as a kind of payback if i had to say why.

Living with them and the rest I had learned to shut myself off from any emotion and watched as when she visited her mum she was crying, she said her house had been robbed, in my head i was laughing and thinking you stupid people,

They covered up abuse that happened so my reply was go and f**k yourselves but in my head.

I ran into my mother after a time and found out she was living close by so i started to visit her, we had a weird bond, it felt more like mates than a mother & son, drinking, smoking.

One evening my biological brother turned up at me mams house and me mam asked us to babysit the younger kids, my half-siblings, wasn't a problem and I remember a bottle of vodka was thrown into the deal and off my mother went on a night out.

It was very late when mother and her boyfriend came home drunk, they walked in shouting at each other, it then escalated and he then

No One Cares

belted my mother right in front of me, I remember being 17, full of hate, anger, a complete distrust of people and unattached from any emotions,

I pulled a knife on him and threatened him that if he ever hit her again or even laid a single finger on her I would kill him, a fight broke out and my mother tried to get in the way of us to break it up.

The whole house erupted into chaos and after a few punches were thrown things calmed for a few minutes, my mother said the police were on the way so I left by the back door into the night, however I was not done yet, this man I had hated for years he had abused me when I had lived with them when I was younger and hurt my mother, he had caused so much pain.

I walked around to the front of the terraced house and started to hit the front door, I had lost all sense of capacity and was just reacting to the situation.

I was goading him to come out and fight me again, thinking back im glad he didn't because i think i would have killed him, the police turned up in full force, they saw I had a knife and surrounded me at a distance, when my mother came out one of them grabbed her I

No One Cares

was so lost in my rage I took a swing a the officer with the knife and he backed off a little.

I waited with knife in hand ready to pounce if any officers came within distance of me, we had made our way around the corner by now and unbeknown to me other officers were waiting around the corner, one came up behind me and all I remember is being floored with such force to the ground and restrained by a lot of officers, i was still raging when they put in the back of a police van and in stepped this hench copper and sat on the bench, being the animal I had or was becoming I taunted the officer which led to him stamping on my ankle and punching me multiple times, again my own fault, I had lost complete control.

I was led to the police cells and left overnight to cool off, in the morning 6 officers walked into the cell, my first thoughts were i was about to get a beating but instead they handcuffed me and led me to a waiting van to be taken to the CDC - Detention Court , I sat in a cell waiting to be processed expecting i was going to prison, I sat there numb, not really thinking about anything, no emotion shown at my situation, a duty solicitor turned up and my foster parent and

No One Cares

social worker turned up at court, I remember the judge asked me if I had anything to say before he makes his final judgement, I took the opportunity to apologize to the officers for my behaviour, I was given a two year suspended sentence and told if I breached that in any way i would serve any remaining time in prison to which I agreed with the judges terms.

I learned to not get arrested but i can honestly say I was no saint during this period nor did i ever go to prison nor have I ever been to prison in any of my life.

Social services paid my foster parents for taking me in, they also paid for holidays which is where i tried to escape in meeting new people, still drinking, taking drugs and behaving like a complete arse, I met this shy girl and had a holiday fling, I remember her dad was on the warpath because i wasn't the type of guy your daughter should bring home, we swapped addresses and after the holiday we wrote to each other, this was before the internet and smartphones.

I returned home still flaunting about with the ladies, one being my mother's friend, we sat in the pub and I invited myself back to her house, I had a certain kind of self confidence in that respect, we got

No One Cares

to her house and her husband was sitting in the kitchen, he worked for a taxi firm but hadn't left for work yet, he saw me and looked at his wife and said "it's like that is it" and walked out and left to go to work, this woman was around 20 years difference to me, we initially left it at that but something kept pulling me back, I don't know what nor can't explain it and it led to me harassing her and becoming an anti-social nuisance to the point her husband came out and punched me on one of those times of a late evening.

When i look back i think i was bored, unguided, left to my own devices so i was out all day or all night with no real structure to my life, it revolved around drink & drugs and women.

After her husband had punched me I filled with rage again and lost my head, he had walked back into the house by now.
I walked up to his car and punched through both side windows with my bare fists, i don't remember doing the neighbours as well but I think that's part of psychosis when you lose all control or capacity of what you're doing, you just react without thinking of any consequences.

No One Cares

The neighbour unfortunately was the local barman who considered himself a local hard man, more like an idiot and more into drugs than I was but to be fair he could handle himself and i was just an out of control kid, he caught up with me a few days later and gave me a beating and threatened to blow my legs off with a gun if I didn't come up with the cash to fix his windows, he's still waiting even now.

I was still writing to this girl I met on holiday and her family invited me down south to visit them so I jumped at the chance to escape my current situation for a while, I had travelled around that much i loved it, I hadn't a place I could really call my home and i didn't have any real attachments to anyone so i went.

One thing I can say about where I was born is the attitude is bred from birth and from the hard lifestyle you need in order to survive there, we will talk to anyone and ive never met a shy person from there in my life, i think it's unheard of.

Down south I was an instant hit with the what I considered to be country bumpkins, a farmer style area to me being from a massive

No One Cares

city, all this countryside was new to me again, I found it quite relaxing and peaceful, but honestly, I was just looking for a way out of my shit life by any means necessary and would do anything it took to make that happen, if i didn't id have to return back to that life.

The visit went well and everyone seemed to like me but by the end I wanted more so I hinted about moving down here to live nearer to this girl and I then left to head back up north, after many phone calls and more letters between ourselves her father offered for me to live with them, I was shocked but jumped at the chance to escape, on the day of leaving this shithole of my life i woke up early with a train ticket booked, I quickly packed a bag and walked downstairs but my foster parent was already up and came down when I was in the middle of writing her a note, my foster parent said "You're not coming back are you"? I replied "No" and took my bag and left without looking back, not once.

I had broken free from the corrupt care system that was supposed to look after and help steer me in the right direction of life but had failed, all I could think about "I Was Free" , not knowing what I was

No One Cares

heading for, not that I actually cared, once i was on that train i put my birth place out of my head and it was gone forever.

For three years I lived with this girl and her family became quite close, i was working and even on the way to a manager role within a supermarket and even took a second job, I paid my way for living with them but I think the amount of work took me away from her too much and things started to fall apart, I began drinking quite heavily and even going into work still pissed from the night before, it wasn't too bad because i started early so I could get the work done before customers came in, this went on for about six months our relationship broke down even though we lived in the same house we became distant, she didn't return from work one day instead had phoned to say she was staying at her aunties and not coming home, so i was asked to leave.

The next part of this taught me a lot about myself and my behaviour towards other people with no one to rely on but your own instincts in order to survive, I had to make a choice, live it or change it.

I was homeless, i sofa surfed for a while through work colleagues but this wasn't good enough, it affected my job so i quit, i was then

No One Cares

on the streets, no home, no job, no family or friends to turn too, I could have quite easily given up, my mind completely broke, after many nights on the streets sleeping rough, freezing my nuts off watching people pass by without a care in the world to who i was, do you know how upsetting that was, i was so jealous of people who all seemed to have good lives, why didn't I, what was wrong with me, i finally ended up in a hostel and given a warm bed & food, that's when i actually broke down mentally at everything that had happened throughout my life, drink was my escape to survive, initially it took me around six months to snap out of my breakdown, on medication and attempts to end my life using tablets, a friend saw me whilst i was dizzy & disoriented because i had taken too many tablets with their help i managed to walk half way to a hospital but then had to lay down on a bench, i continued to puke pulling the lining from my stomach, a member of staff was called from the hostel and she gave me a lift to the hospital, i survived again because good people did their jobs properly.

I was so lost in my head now that i learned the hard way to deal with what life throws at you, my path was difficult but managed to make some friends in the hostel, I even got a flat from there but i

No One Cares

destroyed it because I couldn't support myself and honestly i couldn't look after myself, after a couple of years I went off working with some gypsies and began working for them building driveways for homeowners, they were dodgy and a lot of money changed hands, i wasn't naive at this point and ensured i got my share of money.
They even bought me my own caravan and we lived on a site for a while, i worked during the day and drank myself stupid at night and effectively disappeared from the known world.

I decided I had had enough of this life so i stole a van from them and left to go back up north, but my inexperience I crashed it into a car, i was then arrested by the police so i told them it belongs to the gypsies, it was untraceable for some reason so they let me off.

I got a train back up north and lived on the streets up their, i found food via charities that were known to the homeless whilst i searched for my dad, I found him and stayed with him for a couple of days but

No One Cares

his paranoia set in and he accused me of stealing from him and he kicked me out, so again I was on the streets.

I was more aware now how to survive on the streets, or so i thought, I don't write this for any sympathy I just want people to acknowledge everything that i have had to endure,
I made a mistake and mixed with the wrong crowd, I have never told anyone this so whoever reads this that knows me please don't pity me, don't hug me, don't feel sorry for me, as a man ive found it very difficult to even discuss this, I was set upon by a group of men and raped, I was so broken in my own head, I felt so weak, but I've always said to myself it will never happen ever again, I would kill anyone who tries.

Its taught me about my own security, privacy, safety, so I live my life now in a very private way that may seem weird to some but it's very calculated in what I do, I distrust people.
Before you even talk to me I've already read your body language and know when you're lying or wanting to say something, anyone apart from my missus dosn't know an awful lot about me, it's how i protect myself, I may seem cold and uncaring at times but i care

No One Cares

more than anyone knows, but that can make me vulnerable in a way because people take advantage of it, I drank heavily to cover up my real feelings, i went from woman to woman cheating on them and travelled up and down this country looking for something, looking for a life, looking for a reason to exist, a reason to not kill myself.

I have had to take a long hard look at myself since stopping drinking and doing drugs and my mental health was seen for what it is, I struggle every day with even little things other people take for granted, im jealous of other people who have their own families because it makes me keep questioning why didn't mine want me.

I put it to my mother, i even offered her to stay with us and live a better life down here but she's still drinking and continues to live a lie and has manipulated the family she lives around that I'm a bad person, because my brother tried to kill our mother by way of poisoning her and they presume im exactly like him, I'm not, he is a very dangerous person to be around which i do not want to get into, other than he's been to prison for armed robbery & kidnapping people, being a member of a well known gang related crew who have links to very high associations.

No One Cares

We imprint onto children, everything I did was because i was taught the wrong way of what it means to be a decent human being, so I can not regret what I did on that part, but I do regret what I did by my own choices, I made mistakes ive held my hands up and faced the consequences of those times so can a person be held accountable for such times ?

That's still debated even today studies into psychosis to prove a person lacks capacity in certain difficult situations, how can they be held accountable if they don't fully understand what they're doing or have done.

That's why i believe those in charge of looking after children should be held accountable and that shouldn't matter if it's the parents or any authority associated with the child.

I met my good lady who is now my wife and she already had two children, a boy and a girl, we went on to have three of our own children, two boys and a girl, this is my family we've created, this family shows me what real love within a family is supposed to be like, I am soft on my children because I wouldn't ever want them to experience anything i've had to endure, but support my missus who

No One Cares

is a lot stricter than me, and we teach our children to be confident, speak up for themselves if wronged or abused, look out for each other, look out for family and friends, one has joined military services of which we are very proud of because at school he had the world record for detentions, we all learn at our own pace.

It's been very difficult at times for myself and my missus because I worried about her leaving me and things going on in my head, my own thoughts playing against me, I expect people to give up on me, hell I've given up on myself sometimes as well, but my missus is someone who has stood her ground with me and stood at my side when idiots tried starting trouble, we're like chalk & cheese, I have my own mind, my missus has her own mind, neither controls the other and we try to work together, sometimes we disagree or I haven't heard something she's said because im easily lost or distracted, but when it comes to being parents my missus is a great parent.

I know we've lived in between work & benefits but we manage to always provide food, drink, warmth, clothing, toys, even love and affection & time for all the children, I followed the welfare reforms as

No One Cares

part of the work i was doing for a charity so we could advise the service users on the coming changes as part of the Universal Credit introduction, which is why I still get people asking for assistance in completing their forms or advice on such matters, I personally don't want hand-outs, I really wish my life was so different, that I could afford my own house or had my own business and didn't have to worry about money, I accept where I am and the hand I've been dealt, but it's taught me not to judge anyone else, other people's income is naff all to do with me so I'm always confused when people keep asking about mine, it's none of your business, I answer to who I need to, when necessary but as for the rest I don't really think about.

I've learned to drive and own a car, I like to think I'm a good driver as no points or speeding fines since gaining my license, I also think because my mind races at 50 miles an hour I am more alert through anxiety when driving, I love driving because it offers me freedom, it allows me to get to places, take the children to visit places, but it also protects me because I still worry about being around people so I struggle to even walk down a normal street, my children just say

No One Cares

I'm lazy but I know it's because they don't understand the reasons of this.

That makes me think especially with my own experiences that school isn't for everyone, yes children need education but when you have complex issues such as mental health or learning disabilities then mainstream schools do not offer enough help because it is limited by lack of funding.

I have since attending specific meetings to get people to think about better funding. children's schools & services because later on there will be fewer adults requiring services such as mental healthcare which does drain local authority and NHS funding, it shouldn't matter about money as to if a child has a good life or not, there needs to be better support throughout, there's a simple card system for children experiencing anxiety they show the card to the teacher and can leave the room without having to explain the reasoning which in itself can cause conflicts, as part of my studies into social care i hit on the www technique of talking to suicidal people, its a form of open questioning that offers them a chance to respond, i found that worked with a lot of challenging people, especially those who struggle with verbal communication or lack of.

No One Cares

They were able to respond clearly when they were confident enough and trusted you enough to do so, over time you then build up a good level of trust, but it's also important to allow them to grow and be independant and I proved this method worked because a client required less support from a psychiatrist & psychologist as they grew in self confidence going from an institutionalised state into a member of the community making their own choices in their life, even going shopping for someone with a learning disability or a mental health condition can be an extremely challenging experience for that person just in general as there's billions of other humans to contend with, then throw into that those who mistreat such people and try to bully them,

That's where the fight or flight comes in, depending on the situation depends on the vulnerable person, in my time in social care i've had to stop clients hitting members of the public that could have caused them to get into trouble or the member of the public could have reacted aggressively back, so you gain a sense of responsibility when supporting a person.

No One Cares

I was able to put myself in the shoes of the people i was supporting, that comes from empathy, an understanding of what it's like for them, living in care services can be very solitary for a lot of people, family may not always be around.

Care might be just 15 minutes a day to a full on 24/7 depending on the person's needs, just because the support is in the same building it still doesn't offer the same level of closeness a family setting offers, this is why any person in care should have family involved because ive seen the massive difference in a person when families around.

I was once told a person with autism will struggle to express emotion from someone who saw them every three months or so but when you're with that person nearly every shift you see they can & do express all kinds of emotions as well as affection towards staff & people they care about, I work in adult services and it's amazing work in what we can do, I would recommend doing it at some point in life, I even helped a person consider it despite her thinking she had no experience, I reminded her you live with a sister who was on the autistic spectrum, "oh yes" she said, people don't think about

No One Cares

that, we just live with it and generally get on with life without much thought.

Take mental health, attitudes still need to change towards it, not everyone is dangerous to be around, but unless you require the services to help you do you take an interest in these services before then? A lot of people don't and that's why it's important to raise awareness of mental health groups that do offer support, there's many, it shouldn't require a person attempt to end their life before people step in to help, that could be your family member, one of your mates or even a work colleague, just listening to them could be enough to save them.

I've learned every life serves a purpose and doesn't matter if it's good or bad, you have to decide what kind of person you're going to be, just like I have done.

I am the root of my family tree, my family line was broken and is reborn through the family I created, I have since sought help and support through mental health services and have been in and out of work, the point I want to make here is that I keep trying, I may give

No One Cares

up at times but I don't give up on life, my mind is chaotic at times, I get confused, im forgetful, I can start a conversation on one thing and completely talk about something else, I drive my missus insane sometimes but she has stuck by me throughout and I can't express enough how much that means to me.

I went through mental health services and found a charity that did peer support, basic training in how to support others, using lived experience, I found it helped me because i was victimising myself and my thoughts were defeating me from within, I found my purpose through them to help people, I learned a lot about benefits by having to claim them myself, I wasn't born into money, i have no child trust fund, everything i have i have worked hard for it when i am able to work.

I loved supporting other people, after doing the peer support i wanted to do it full time so i found a company willing to take me on, I started at the bottom, I studied and have since acquired my level three in social care as well as gaining my academic school grades through other courses because if you remember I dropped out of

No One Cares

school early, i was great with clients because I could connect really well with them.

I had so much empathy towards them and I learned to become a more professional person towards such things, I worked my way up to management level and even attended tribunals, MoJ , CPA meetings on behalf of people and made a difference to their lives, I am very tough but caring, as long as the whole team plays their part it will work, as a manager I tried to inspire their growth, be it the clients and my staff, listen to them all and above all support them to the best of your abilities.

I get so upset when another care home is on the news for people abusing clients, even today in 2019 abuse is still going on, we as a society need to work together and start changing things, we need to listen more instead of dictating, we need to put people first , profits will always come if you do a good job.

I still live with my illness, some days I manage it well , others not so much but I am surrounded by good people who i live in hope really

No One Cares

care about me, because I care about them, my mental prison is breaking as I look more inwards so i've sought further help because i still feel bitter towards my past and i don't want the raging child to break out who is angry for being abused and treated lesser than an animal at times, i've written this so i can put all this behind me and live the good life I now have with my wife and my family.

I've since found out my original foster parents have passed away some years ago, my biological father passed away and if my mother continues with her life drinking it won't be too long before she goes, because of threats made towards me by other family members i won't be allowed to her funeral.
I made a choice after years of chasing for my mothers love & affections I realised were wasted efforts on my part I stopped & I cut her off, she did manage to let me know about my dad but I think there was some motive behind that too cause an argument between myself and my brother which never happened, I can't help her come to terms with what's happened in her life, she has to take those steps, I have to focus on myself & my family.

No One Cares

Too anyone in child services or supporting those in child care services or even in everyday life please listen to the children, look for the signs because they may be scared to speak up about abuse, a quiet child may be scared, shy or nervous, intervene, never give up on any of them even if they kick off, that's when they need you the most, be the light they lack to show them the way, be a force of good, encourage them to speak up, reassure them it's absolutely ok to do so and ensure them they will be listened too and taken seriously.

Too any youngster who feels you're alone, it may seem like that but you're definitely not alone,
i know it can be confusing having to speak out about family or someone you may know that is abusing you, but you're strong enough to do that, and I would do all I can to enforce that by asking everyone to protect all children through this book.

No matter how dark the world gets just remember it's easier to see the light when darkness surrounds us, I really hope people who know me will understand me a bit more now.

No One Cares

I'm not a bad person, I was crying out for attention, affection, acknowledgment from people and wanting someone to tell me my world had not ended, no Superman or Batman ever came to save me, yes i've done some bad things but i learned from it all and know I will continue as best as I can to help others and stop anyone else having to go through anything like this life,

I live day to day, I live with no plans, I do want to become a local councillor so I can help people within the community to have a good life, but also have a good place for my children to grow up in, so I'm taking steps on this path as well as growing my network of contacts and trying to use my story to help people open up and know you can still have a life even after walking through hell on earth whilst being consumed every day by the flames.

If this book saves even one life, I would be so happy because I know one day that life no matter what path they take will help be a part of our continuing journey called life, I would also just like people to acknowledge what my life has been like.

No One Cares

I'm no expert, yes I've studied and life taught me loads, I don't want to pretend this will solve all the world's problems because it won't, and other people with their own experiences may differ from mine, there is no manual to living a life, we learn as we go, even as adults we're always learning, so take from this what you want, if it helps then great, if it opens your eyes to a bigger picture then great. Just be a good person.

Everyone should care in a world where No One Cares.

Pete.

Printed in Great Britain
by Amazon